WHO, WHAT, WHY?

WHAT WAS
THE CROSS?

DANIKA COOLEY

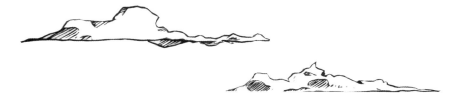

10 9 8 7 6 5 4 3 2 1
Copyright © Danika Cooley 2025
Paperback ISBN: 978-1-5271-1280-3
ebook ISBN: 978-1-5271-1337-4

Published by
Christian Focus Publications,
Geanies House, Fearn, Tain, Ross-shire,
IV20 1TW, Scotland, U.K.
www.christianfocus.com
email: info@christianfocus.com

Printed and bound by Bell and Bain, Glasgow

Cover design by Catriona Mackenzie
Illustrations by Martyn Smith

Scripture quotations are from The Holy Bible, English Standard Version, copyright © 2001 by Crossway Bibles, a publishing ministry of Good News Publishers. Used by permission. All rights reserved. ESV Text Edition: 2011.

All rights reserved. No part of this publication may be reproduced, stored in a retrieval system, or transmitted, in any form, by any means, electronic, mechanical, photocopying, recording or otherwise without the prior permission of the publisher or a licence permitting restricted copying. In the U.K. such licences are issued by the Copyright Licensing Agency, 4 Battlebridge Lane, London, SE1 2HX. www.cla.co.uk

TABLE OF CONTENTS

Chapter One: The Mystery of the Cross 7

Chapter Two: War in the Garden 16

Chapter Three: Blood of the Lamb 24

Chapter Four: Messengers who Spoke for God 32

Chapter Five: Standing Trial in God's Court 42

Chapter Six: Arrival of the God-Man 50

Chapter Seven: The Mission Jesus Accepted 59

Chapter Eight: Victory on the Cross 68

Chapter Nine: Living in God's Kingdom 76

Timeline 84

Works Consulted 87

Dedication

To the Reader (That's you!)
May you know, love, and follow Jesus,
our magnificent Savior.

THE AUTHOR

Danika Cooley and her husband, Ed, are committed to leading their children to live for the glory of God. Danika has a passion for equipping parents to teach the Bible and Christian history to their kids. She is the author of *Help Your Kids Learn and Love the Bible; When Lightning Struck!: The Story of Martin Luther; Bible Investigators: Creation; Wonderfully Made: God's Story of Life from Conception to Birth*, and the *Who, What, Why?* series about the history of our faith. Danika's three year Bible survey curriculum, Bible Road Trip™, is used by families around the world. Weekly, she encourages tens of thousands of parents to intentionally raise biblically literate children. Danika is a homeschool mother of four with a Bachelor of Arts degree from the University of Washington. Find her at ThinkingKidsBlog.org.

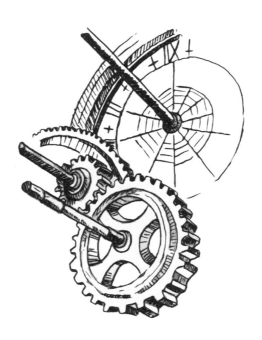

THE MYSTERY
OF THE CROSS

Have you ever seen a picture of the gears inside an old-fashioned clock? Wheels with teeth spin slowly around, anchored in time and space, pushing interconnected toothy disks to the next spot in their rotation. The gears are woven together, each one impacting the next. That is how history works as well. As each person acts out their life, other lives are impacted and turned. Events and movements click into place before spinning us to a new time, a new place, and a new event.

This interconnected overlap of people, events, and movements is exactly what makes history so fascinating. The more you learn about the happenings of the past, the more you will see the invisible gears connecting events together, and you will recognize the ways in which those matters affect your life today. Even more important, the more you learn about our great God and his plan for our salvation, the more you will see his hand in our story.

Of all the events which have occurred in the expanse of human history, not one is more important than the crucifixion of Jesus Christ. A cross was a wooden torture device invented by the Persians in the time of Ezra and then used widely in the Roman era. When you hear or read of the Cross in a Christian context it is referring to a specific event. It refers to the work that Jesus did on that wooden structure.

The Cross is the most important event in all of human history because it is the moment when Jesus, who is God the Son and the Son of God , paid for the sins of all who believe in him. Sin makes us enemies of God. Not only did Jesus bring about the forgiveness of sin for all believers, but at the Cross Jesus also made his followers friends of God instead of his enemies. There's more. At the Cross, Jesus conquered sin and death for all eternity.

Now, Jesus is often two things at once. Jesus is:

- Both God the Son and the Son of God.
- Both fully God and fully man.
- Both the Creator of the Universe and born of a woman whom he created.

In all of history, these things can only be said of Jesus. There is a mystery to these truths. It's not that we can't be certain that what God says is true, but the mystery is that we can not understand exactly how it is true. We can, however, understand what God has revealed to us through his Word so that we can know Jesus and be saved forever. So, we may not understand every mystery about God, nor understand why a truth is so, because we are just people and God is God.

We are a little like grasshoppers trying to understand a giraffe. We can see only a little bit of what is real. But we know that God's Word is trustworthy and correct. So, we learn what God says, and we know that what he says is true. We believe him because he is God.

You know that the Cross is the most important event in all of history. It is the most important event in the Bible, too. In fact, over and over again the stories in the Bible point us toward Jesus and toward the sacrifice he made for us on the Cross. Once you see how the Cross shows up in God's Word, you will notice how all of the Old Testament history points forward to the Cross. All of the New Testament points to the work Jesus did on the Cross too.

After Jesus was crucified, resurrected, and then rose to heaven, the apostle Paul wrote in his letter to the Colossians, "And you, who were dead in your trespasses and the uncircumcision of your flesh, God made alive together with him, having forgiven us all our trespasses, by canceling the record of debt that stood against us with its legal demands. This he set aside, nailing it to the cross" (Colossians 2:13-14).

The Bible is the story of God's great plan for salvation. Paul's words to the Colossians tell us that Jesus carried out God's salvation plan on the Cross. We are all sinners, and the punishment for our sin is death. But, the sins of all who believe in Jesus and turn away from sin (repent), are nailed to the Cross.

The work Jesus did on the Cross to free his people from their sins was planned before the beginning of the earth. The cross alone was just wood, and it could not have accomplished anything without Jesus. Only Jesus, the Son of God, could be miraculously born as fully God and fully man. Only Jesus lived a perfect life. Only Jesus took the punishment for the sin of every believer in him so that we could be forgiven for our rebellion against God.

This is the story of God's great plan for salvation through faith in Jesus, who—by the grace of God—died in the place of sinners on the Cross. It is the story of how Jesus conquered sin and death. It's the story of the greatest event in all of history—the one that can change your life for all of eternity.

HOW THE CROSS BECAME OUR SYMBOL

After Jesus ascended to heaven, Christians wanted a symbol for their faith. Early attempts included a peacock to show we will live forever and the palm leaf awarded to winning athletes to show our victory in Christ. Eventually, Christians settled on a cross as the symbol for their faith.

Around 170 years after Jesus' resurrection, the theologian Tertullian wrote that Christians drew the cross on their forehead before every action as a way to remember what Jesus has done for us. After the Reformation, the Puritans stopped tracing the cross on their foreheads, concerned it was superstitious. Today, many Christians still wear a cross necklace as a reminder that Jesus died to save them from their sins.

WAR IN
THE GARDEN

No one created God, and God is three Persons in one God. The three Persons of our one God—called the Trinity—are God the Father, God the Son, and God the Holy Spirit. Now, together with our Heavenly Father and the Holy Spirit, Jesus—God the Son—created everything. God created the heavens, and he made the earth with frightening sea creatures, colorful birds, and massive land animals. God made a beautiful garden,

Eden, and placed the very first people he made—Adam and Eve—in the garden. The world God made was a perfect paradise. It was the very last place you would ever expect to find a war.

Before there was a war in the garden, there was a revolt in heaven. You see, one of God's created angels—Satan—was proud of his beauty and his splendor, so he rebelled against his Creator. Then, God threw Satan—also called the devil—out of heaven. Satan took other rebellious angels with him, and they became demons, who are evil spirits. Because Satan could never win a war against his Creator God, he waged a war against God's creatures.

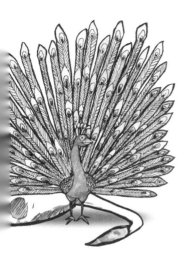

Back in the garden, God told Adam, "You may surely eat of every tree of the garden, but of the tree of the knowledge of good and evil you shall not eat, for in the day that you eat of it you shall surely die" (Genesis 2:16-17). There was no sin, death, or pain in God's good world. That was about to change.

Into the perfect, sinless garden walked a shrewd beast of the field, a serpent. "Hey," he said to Eve, "did God actually tell you not to eat fruit from any tree of the garden?" Is that what God said to Adam? No, it's not, and the crafty serpent knew it.

Eve didn't even blink over a walking snake talking to her. She didn't seem to wonder why he asked her about God's rule. Instead Eve replied, "God told us not to eat fruit from the tree in the middle of the garden. We can't even touch it, or we will die." Do you see what Eve did there? She added to what God said.

"Oh, you won't die," slithered the slippery snake. "God knows you'll eat the fruit of the tree and you'll be like God. Your eyes will be opened and you'll know good and evil." The servant-of-Satan serpent tempted Eve to sin—and so she did. After Eve ate the forbidden fruit, she handed it to Adam and he ate it too.

Now, sin is rebellion against God. Our God is holy and just and without sin, so when we break one of God's rules, our sin separates us from him. It is very sad news that the punishment for sin is death. When God's people sinned by eating fruit from the tree of the knowledge of good and evil, sin entered God's good world. Death entered, too.

Adam and Eve instantly knew that they were naked, so they sewed fig leaves together to make clothes. Then they hid when God came to walk with them. God asked Adam and Eve what they had done.

Nobody accepted the blame. Eve blamed the snake, Adam blamed Eve, and he even blamed God.

No matter who we blame, there are always consequences for our sin. Sin meant Adam and Eve's bodies would one day die, so God's people were sent out of the garden and angels guarded the entrance so they could not return. God also said that having babies would be painful for women and they would struggle to submit in marriage. Men would struggle to grow food and feed their families.

In Genesis 3:14-15, God said to the serpent: "Because you have done this, cursed are you above all livestock and above all beasts of the field; on your belly you shall go, and dust you shall eat all the days of your life. I will put enmity between you and the woman, and between your offspring and her offspring; he shall bruise your head, and you shall bruise his heel."

That was the beginning of a war all through the Bible. Anyone who does not follow Jesus is the child of the serpent. When Jesus was born to Mary, he became both fully God and fully man, the offspring of the woman. Until God creates a new heaven and new earth (which will be free from sin) there will be a war between the followers of Satan and the followers of Jesus.

God promised that Satan would bruise Jesus' heel, and he did. After all, the King of the Universe was murdered on a cross. Even though Jesus died, it was just like a bruise. For, Jesus rose from the dead to live forever.

God also said that Jesus would crush Satan's head. When Jesus went to the Cross and died, it looked like Satan had won. Jesus died on the Cross to save his people—his offspring—from sin and death by taking their punishment on himself. That day at the Cross, Jesus won the war against sin and death—for all Jesus' people will be resurrected to live forever with him. At the Cross, Satan's head was crushed.

DEAD IN YOUR TRESPASSES

Colossians 2:13a says, "And you, who were dead in your trespasses…." Our trespasses are our sins against God. God warned Adam that if he ate the forbidden fruit, he would die. Indeed, when Adam and Eve rebelled against God, sin and death entered the world. All people die eventually, but Christians will be raised to eternal life with Jesus on an entirely new, sinless earth.

Before Jesus saves us from our sins and makes us spiritually alive, we are in a bad situation, indeed. You see, before we are saved, we are spiritually dead—and dead people are unable to choose to follow Christ. That's why we need a Savior to make us alive so that we can repent and be saved.

WHO, WHAT, WHY?

BLOOD OF
THE LAMB

God's curse on the serpent is the first time that the story of salvation in the Bible points us to the Cross, but it isn't the last time. Do you remember the story of the Exodus? More than 2,500 years after God promised that Jesus would crush Satan's head, the Israelites were enslaved in Egypt. They cried out to God for rescue, so God sent Moses to confront

the Egyptian Pharoah. Over and over, Moses told Pharoah that God said, "Let my people go." Time and again, Pharoah said, "No!"

So, God sent plagues on the people of Egypt, who sinfully worshiped many fake gods and even thought their Pharaoh was a god. First God turned water to blood. Then, he sent swarms of frogs, gnats, and flies. Next, the cows, horses, and camels died. God sent painful boils before raining down hail and fire. Locusts ate the green plants of Egypt, followed by three days of complete darkness. Still, Pharaoh's heart was the

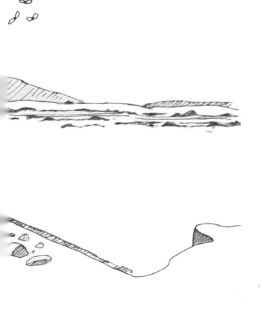

hardest of hard. He would not let God's people go. So, God threatened to send one more plague, the death of every firstborn son in Egypt. Yet, the Pharaoh still told God, "No! I will not let your people go."

The very night of God's judgment on the people of Egypt, God saved the Israelites through a spotless lamb. You see, God had each family sacrifice a perfect little year-old male lamb and paint its blood on the doorposts of each home. It seems terrible that a lamb died in the place of God's people, doesn't it? Sin is a horrid thing with awful consequences.

That night, the Lord passed over the land, bringing death on the firstborn son in every Egyptian household. But, every home covered in the blood of

the lamb was spared. Early the next morning, as the people of Egypt wept, the Israelites packed up and left slavery forever, setting out to follow God across the wilderness to the Promised Land.

It is important that we know just who the Bible tells us God is. God is holy—that means he is set apart from his creatures. God is without sin. Also, God is just—that means he is fair and righteous in the way he judges us. While our holy God cannot tolerate sin, he loves us so much that he makes a way for us to be forgiven—saved—so that we can be with him forever.

In Jewish life, sacrifices happened over and over again. Each time blood was shed for sin, it pointed

forward to Jesus' work on the Cross. Today, we say that these rituals in the Old Testament, like the Passover feast, were like shadows. Each shadow was a vague picture of the truth that was to come later. The sacrificial lamb was a substitute for the sinner. You see, the lamb died in the place of the sinner, just as Jesus would one day die in the place of believers at the Cross.

In the Old Testament, the Passover lamb was a substitute for the Israelites—it took their place. Even

though our sin requires death, God does not require our eternal death for our own sin. Instead, he allowed a perfect lamb to shed its blood in the place of each sinner who believed in God and in his promise of a coming Savior.

Nearly 1,500 years after the first Passover, Jesus was just beginning his ministry on earth. At the same time, a prophet named John the Baptist was preaching in the wilderness, calling people to repent to get ready for the coming Messiah. When John saw Jesus walking toward him, he cried out, "Behold, the Lamb of God, who takes away the sin of the world!" (John 1:29b). John the Baptist meant that Jesus would be the substitute for every sinner who believes in Jesus and repents. He is the Lamb who takes away our sin.

Three years later, Jesus was eating with his disciples at a celebration of the Passover feast the night before his crucifixion. Jesus thanked his Father God for the bread and broke it into pieces, handing each of his disciples a piece. "This is my body, which is given for you. Do this in remembrance of me" (Luke 22:19). The disciples ate the bread, then Jesus passed around a cup of wine, and said, "This cup that is poured out for you is the new covenant in my blood" (Luke 22:20).

Jesus was telling his disciples that he would stand in their place and take the punishment for their sin as he died on the Cross. His body and his blood would be substituted for theirs. Because Jesus paid the price for the sins of his people, we can be saved from eternal death. In fact, Christians will live forever with Jesus. Today, we still take Communion with bread and the juice of grapes to remember that on the day the Passover lambs were killed in Jerusalem, the perfect, sinless Lamb of God took away the sin of the world.

THE UNCIRCUMCISION OF YOUR FLESH

Before believing in Jesus we are dead in our sins. Then Paul wrote in Colossians 2:13a, "...and the uncircumcision of your flesh..." It can be easy for our brains to skip over parts of the Bible we don't understand, can't it? It's worthwhile to figure out what the words of God that were written for us mean.

God told Moses that males must be circumcised to show they belonged to God. Removing a piece of skin symbolized cutting off sin in order to be set aside as holy to God. When we are dead in our sins, we are not set aside for God. We are 'un-circumcised' which just means that we have not yet turned from sin to follow Jesus.

WHO, WHAT, WHY?

MESSENGERS
WHO SPOKE FOR GOD

After the Israelites held their first Passover feast with their doorposts covered in the blood of a pure lamb, God led them out of slavery in Egypt during the Exodus. Now, the Israelites were grumbling grumblers who often complained against God, just as we do sometimes, so their journey to the new land God promised them took a really long time. Eventually, their children entered the Promised Land and settled down, having families, worshiping God, and obeying their kings.

Actually, sometimes the Israelites forgot to worship God, or neglected to worship him as he wants to be worshiped. Instead, they did what was right in their own eyes. Their kings sometimes acted the same way. Then, God would send messengers—called prophets—to speak his words to the Israelites. God would remind his people that they must worship only him. He also warned them to worship him the right way, the way God himself told his people to worship him. Then, God told his people to love and serve each other with justice, as God had outlined justice in his law.

The prophets had another message they shared with God's people and with the kings. You see, God's messengers told his people more about the coming

Messiah—the Savior. The prophets said that Jesus would be from the tribe of Judah, a descendent of Jacob—the father of the Israelites. God's prophets also told the Israelites that Jesus would be born of a virgin, that he would be born in Bethlehem, that he would speak in parables, and that he would ride a donkey. The prophets shared God's words about Jesus' death and resurrection, too. They said he would be a Savior for all people.

While God sent many prophets to speak to the Jews, his prophet Isaiah began sharing messages from God with the kings of Judah. At that time Judah was in the southern kingdom of Israel. It was just about 700 years after the very first Passover. In chapters 52 and 53 of his book, the prophet Isaiah shared a long message from God about the coming of Jesus. You can read the whole prophecy in your Bible.

Imagine being an Israelite in the days of the kings and hearing the words of Isaiah about God's suffering servant. Isaiah called out to the people, saying:

> Surely he has borne our griefs
> and carried our sorrows;
> yet we esteemed him stricken,
> smitten by God, and afflicted.
> But he was pierced for our transgressions;

he was crushed for our iniquities;
upon him was the chastisement that
brought us peace,
and with his wounds we are healed.
All we like sheep have gone astray;
we have turned—every one—to his own way;
and the Lord has laid on him
the iniquity of us all (Isaiah 53:4-6).

Many Israelites were expecting God to send a mighty king to rule them. But God was telling them that he would send a "man of sorrows" (v.3)" to carry sins and to be punished by God for sin—or rebellion against our holy God. Then, God told his people that the Messiah would be pierced and he would bring peace with God to those who believed in him. The Messiah would be wounded, but those who trusted in him would be healed spiritually. That seems pretty mysterious, doesn't it? God does things his own way, because he is God.

In Isaiah 53:12b, we read:

> ... because he poured out his soul to death
> and was numbered with the transgressors;
> yet he bore the sin of many,
> and makes intercession for the transgressors.

First, Jesus bore our sin on the Cross as if he himself was the sinner, even though he never sinned. Then, he paid the penalty for the sins of all who believe in him, confess their belief, and repent. Last, he died the death that his followers should have died. Jesus was

struck by God for the sins or trespasses of his people—he was wounded for their rebellion. That is the work Jesus did on the Cross.

Why did Jesus do this? He died on the Cross willingly and on purpose as a part of God's great plan for salvation. The Bible tells us that God the Father loves us. So, he sent God the Son to be born fully God and fully human, to live a perfect life and to die a sacrificial death, all so our sin can be removed. Those who trust in Jesus Christ are no longer separated from God. In fact, Christians have God the Holy Spirit living in them!

God sent the prophet Isaiah to tell the Israelites that Jesus was on the way and that he would die to secure forgiveness for their sins. Because the Israelites were very human, they remembered that a Messiah was coming, but they forgot that he would be put to death for their sins. Instead of God's suffering servant, they waited for a human king who would wage war on earth against their enemies. But, God sent the Lamb of God, the offspring of the woman, to die in our place and to wage war with the serpent on the Cross. God sent his very own Son, Jesus, to be our Savior.

We have all sinned against our holy God, and we all need his forgiveness. Today is the perfect day to ask yourself the two most important questions. Do you believe that Jesus is God the Son, who became man to die on the cross to pay for the sins of those who believe in him, and that he rose from the dead three days later? Will you turn from your sins and follow Jesus so you will become a forgiven child of God? It is important to talk to an adult Christian, like a parent or pastor, about these questions. You can also pray and ask God to help you believe.

GOD MADE US ALIVE IN HIM

Our rebellion against God has made us dead in our trespasses, and our flesh is full of the rottenness of sin—we are uncircumcised and unholy. That's sad news. But, Paul wrote in the third section of Colossians 2:13, that "God made us alive together with him." Jesus rose from the dead and so will Christians.

That is wonderful, amazing, stupendous news! We ought to shout it from the rooftops—or at least from park benches. After Jesus paid the penalty for the sins of all believers, he rose to life in his new, glorified body. When you believe in Jesus, confess your belief, and repent, God makes you alive forever in Jesus. That's the message the prophets came to share.

While the Passover lamb died to spare people the judgment of death, the salvation offered was only temporary. Jesus Christ died so that those who believe in him and turn from their sin can live forever with God. The Lamb of God offers salvation from the slavery of sin for all eternity.

STANDING
TRIAL IN GOD'S COURT

If you are caught breaking the law, you will be arrested. Now, you are likely too young and too obedient to be sentenced as a criminal mastermind, so we will just have to pretend. You would only need to break one law to be arrested and charged with a crime. Then, you would stand trial before being sentenced for your guilt.

In a human courtroom, there is a judge who oversees the trial to make sure that it is just—which means fair, and that everything proceeds according to the rules. The judge also condemns and sentences the guilty person. There is a lawyer who presents the charges against the person on trial—the defendant, and a second lawyer who defends the defendant.

Depending on the laws that are broken, a defendant may end up doing several hours of service for their community or paying a fine. They could also be put

in prison for days, months, or even years. In some countries, in the case of a terrible, done-on-purpose crime that hurts someone badly, a defendant could even be sentenced to die. If you are like most people, you will never stand trial in a court of law, since most people never go out of their way to harm others.

That is not true in God's heavenly court of law. You see, every person will one day stand trial before God. The Bible tells us that God is:

- Our holy Lawmaker. He has given us a set of perfect laws to follow.

- Our just Judge. God knows about every time we have broken his law. He even knows when we break his law in our hearts.

- Our righteous Sentence-Giver. Our crimes against God mean that, just like Adam and Eve in the garden, we are no longer able to live forever with God. Instead, we are sentenced to die physically, and then to die eternally—to live apart from God forever.

When we sin—rebel—against God by breaking his rules, we commit a crime against the Creator of the Universe. That sounds serious, doesn't it? That's because it is. The sentence for our crime is death forever.

What is a crime against God? In the book of Exodus, chapter 20, God gave Moses ten rules, or commandments, for us to live by. God's rules teach us how to love God and love others. The fifth rule, in Exodus 20:12, says: "Honor your father and your mother, that your days may be long in the land that the Lord your God is giving you." Have you ever disobeyed your parents? Have you shown your anger at them by stomping or rolling your eyes? Well, then you've broken rule five. Now, Jesus told us that if we even just break God's law in our hearts, such as with angry or selfish thoughts, then we are guilty before God.

Every single one of us has broken God's law. Romans 3:23 says, "for all have sinned and fall short of the glory of God." We have all committed a crime against God, and we all stand guilty before him. We owe a debt we cannot pay. No amount of good behavior can erase our guilt for the crime we have committed against God.

Back to our imaginary trial. Imagine you are in court, standing trial for a crime you definitely committed, and you are sentenced to death forever. That is terrible news. It's the worst news ever. Still, the sentence would be fair because of the terrible crime you had committed.

Now, suppose your lawyer offers to pay your debt for you. That's right—your lawyer will stand trial in your place, taking the guilt for your crime. Not only that, your lawyer offers to die in your place so that you can live. Amazing! So, the judge erases your debt. Your crime is gone—like it never even happened.

There's even more good news. The judge doesn't just erase the record of your debt. He goes even further and invites you to become a part of his family—one of his beloved children. He brings you home to his mansion to live with him and his big, adopted family forever.

You would be relieved, wouldn't you? Your crime is erased, your sentence is lifted, and you are given the status of a beloved child of the most powerful Judge

in the universe. That is exactly what Jesus has done for all of his followers.

Do you remember Romans 3:23? We are all guilty of failing to obey God's law. Even one single sin separates us from God and convicts us of a crime worthy of death. But Jesus, our God who created the heavens and the earth, took the punishment for the sin of every one of his followers.

That's what the Cross was. It was the place where Jesus became our substitute, taking our punishment so we can have our sins erased. It's hard to believe, but Jesus does even more —he gives his own righteousness to his people. In fact, Jesus stands before God the Father in the heavenly court of law and says the name of everyone who has repented and believed in him. He is our lawyer, confirming our innocence.

OUR TRESPASSES FORGIVEN

After we were dead in our trespasses and unwilling to separate our bodies from sin, how did God then make us alive together with him? Paul explains that God used the Cross to save us, "having forgiven us all our trespasses" (Colossians 2:13d).

Jesus, our perfect substitute, took our place on the Cross and paid the penalty for our sins. What does it mean that he has forgiven all our trespasses? Romans 8:1 says, "There is therefore now no condemnation for those who are in Christ Jesus." When God forgives you, all your sins—past, present, and future—you are forgiven forever. You will want to obey God, though, because the Holy Spirit will live in your heart and rebelling against God will make you sad.

WHO, WHAT, WHY?

ARRIVAL OF THE
GOD-MAN

Around 700 years after God gave the prophet Isaiah a message about the coming Messiah, the angel Gabriel visited a young woman named Mary in Nazareth, in Galilee. At the time, Galilee was a region in the land of Israel, which was ruled by the Roman Empire. Mary and a man named Joseph were legally bound together—engaged to be married.

Now, you probably wonder why an important angel like Gabriel, who stood in the presence of God, would visit a girl in a poor region of a nation taken over by an ever-expanding empire. Mary wondered, too. In fact, when Gabriel said, "Greetings, O favored one, the Lord is with you!" (Luke 1:28), she was puzzled about how she could be favored by the Lord. Mary didn't yet know that God was going to use her life as a part of the most important event in history.

"Do not be afraid, Mary, for you have found favor with God," Gabriel said. "And behold, you will conceive in your womb and bear a son, and you shall call his

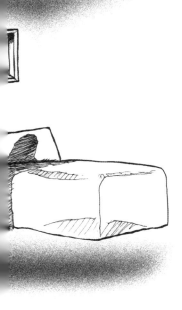

name Jesus. He will be great and will be called the Son of the Most High. And the Lord God will give to him the throne of his father David, and he will reign over the house of Jacob forever, and of his kingdom there will be no end" (Luke 1:30-33). What amazing news! Mary would be the mother of the Son of God—the Messiah, the Savior of all people, the King of the Universe.

Mary wondered how this could be since she was a virgin, and therefore could not be pregnant. Gabriel explained that, through the Holy Spirit, she would give birth to the holy Son of God. Mary trusted God, so she accepted this most mysterious mystery.

Do you know what a miracle is? Well, when God created the earth, he put into place natural laws, such as gravity, and spiritual laws, such as Jesus is the only Savior and we must trust in him. A miracle is an act of God which happens outside of the laws God set up. For instance, when God parted the Red Sea so the Israelites could walk through on dry land, that was a miracle. It was something that could never occur if God himself didn't cause it to happen.

Jesus' birth was also a miraculous miracle. It wasn't a miracle that he was born in Bethlehem after Mary and Joseph traveled there to be counted in a census.

Rather, it was a miracle that a baby was born to a virgin, for Mary had no natural way to have a baby. But, the most amazing miracle was that Jesus was born the Son of God. His Father was Almighty God, and his human mother was a lady from Galilee.

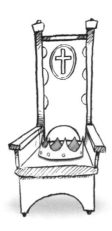

Do you remember that Jesus is often two things at once? Jesus is:

- Both God the Son and the Son of God.
- Both fully God and fully man.
- Both the Creator of the Universe and born of a woman whom he created.

No person on earth is both God and man—except for Jesus. We call this miraculous miracle the Incarnation, the event when God became man. Jesus didn't just step into a human costume. He actually became all-the-way God and all-the-way man for all of eternity. Jesus often referred to himself as the Son of Man in order to let people know that he is the Messiah promised through Adam, through Moses, and through Isaiah. Saying that Jesus is both fully God and fully man can be a mouthful, so some people call Jesus the God-man as a way to remember that Jesus is all-the-way God and all-the-way man.

Are you wondering why God the Son became fully human? Remember, in our courtroom scene the lawyer takes the punishment of the true criminal on himself, paying for the crime of the person accused. Only a sinless human could pay for human sin, and only God is sinless.

Also remember, each one of us owes our Creator God honor and obedience. We have rebelled against him. God is not just holy and just, he is also the King

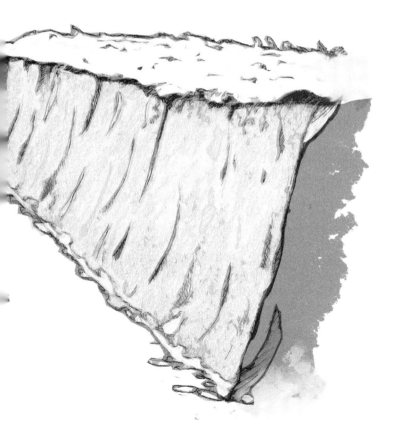

of the Universe. We have all stolen from God the honor and obedience that we owe him, and that's a crime. Can't we pay our own debt? Well, no. We can't repay our debt on our own because we are law-breakers—criminals. We also can't repay the debt anyone else owes. Even your mom or dad can't take your punishment for you.

But, God loves us so much that he sent his Son to pay the debt for us. A human had to pay the penalty for our sin. But, he couldn't be just any human—he had

to be a human without sin. So, Jesus, who is God the Son, became the God-man, born of a virgin. He lived a perfect, sinless life. Even Jesus' private thoughts were sinless!

That's the reason Jesus could pay your debt on the Cross. He is the only man who never sinned because he is the only man who is also God. Jesus becoming the God-man may seem mysterious to us, but that's because the Incarnation is also one of the most miraculous miracles of all time.

OUR RECORD OF DEBT CANCELED

How did God make us alive together with Jesus, having forgiven us all our trespasses? Paul tells us it is, "by canceling the record of debt" (Colossians 2:14a). Romans 6:23 says, "For the wages of sin is death, but the free gift of God is eternal life in Christ Jesus our Lord."

Imagine you borrow money from your brother for ice cream. You may scribble a note saying, "I owe you," promising to repay your debt. If your brother took the note and ripped it in half, that would cancel the debt. The price of our debt to God is so much more than an ice cream bar, and the gift of eternal life with Jesus is so much sweeter.

THE MISSION
JESUS ACCEPTED

A mission is an important assignment or duty. Jesus knew exactly what his mission on earth was to be. In fact, Jesus planned his mission. He came to die on the Cross for our sins.

Where Adam failed in sinning, Jesus succeeded in being righteous. As the Lamb of God, Jesus' sacrifice covered our sins once-and-for-all. As our prophet who speaks God's words, Jesus came to teach us about salvation and living as a part of God's kingdom. Because he is God, everything Jesus did and said was perfect.

Jesus came, too, to crush the head of the serpent. Now, there really wasn't a battle between Satan and Jesus. After all, Jesus, who is the King of the Universe, created Satan. Instead, Satan waged war against Jesus' people, working to harm us. On the Cross, Jesus suffered as he died, so Satan was able to bruise his heel. But, Jesus crushed Satan's head when he forgave the sin of all his followers, winning the battle over death and sin.

Throughout his three-year ministry, Jesus told his disciples that he came to die. Once, in the village of Caesarea Philippi, Jesus taught his disciples that he would suffer and be killed by the Jewish religious leaders—the elders, chief priests, and scribes. But, Jesus promised his disciples he would rise from the dead in three days. His disciples, especially Peter, did not like this teaching at all. In fact, Peter told Jesus to stop speaking this way. Jesus corrected Peter for thinking like a man—the offspring of Satan. Instead, Christians should care about God's plans, thinking like the offspring of God.

Later, as Jesus and his disciples walked through Galilee, he told them he would be handed over to men who would kill him but he would rise three days later. Now, the disciples didn't like this but they were afraid, so they didn't say anything.

Finally, as Jesus and his disciples walked toward Jerusalem for the last time, Jesus spoke to his closest disciples, the Twelve. "See, we are going up to Jerusalem, and the Son of Man will be delivered over to the chief priests and the scribes, and they will condemn him to death and deliver him over to the Gentiles. And they will mock him and spit on

him, and flog him and kill him. And after three days he will rise" (Mark 10:33-34), Jesus told them.

On the evening of the Passover, Jesus and his disciples gathered to celebrate God's redemption of his people with the yearly feast. Elsewhere, the Jewish priests, elders, and scribes had been plotting how to kill Jesus. You see, they were offspring of the serpent and they loved their power much more than they loved God. They knew that Jesus claimed to be the Christ—the Messiah. They had seen the miraculous signs Jesus did, such as healing people and casting out demons. The priests did not like it. They did not like it at all.

As Jesus and his disciples gathered together, he washed their feet. Then, Jesus taught his disciples to remember his broken body and his shed blood which was to free them from sin by taking bread and wine in a special ceremony or meal. Today Christians call this meal Communion, or the Lord's Supper. Once they sang a hymn, Jesus' friends followed him across the Brook Kidron to the Mount of Olives, out to the Garden of Gethsemane. It was a place where Jesus often went to pray to his Father God in the Holy Spirit.

Jesus told the disciples to ask God to keep them from temptation. Then, away from the group, Jesus

knelt and prayed, "Father, if you are willing, remove this cup from me. Nevertheless, not my will, but yours, be done" (Luke 22:42). What did Jesus mean when he asked God to remove this cup from him? Jesus meant God's cup of wrath that the prophets wrote about in the Old Testament. God's wrath is his punishment. At the Cross, Jesus would suffer God's wrath in the place of his followers—all past, present, and future believers.

The Bible says Jesus was full of sorrow, that he was troubled, and that he was in so much agony that he sweat great drops, like blood. So, the Father sent an angel from heaven to strengthen Jesus.

Now, Jesus' disciples were sleeping rather than praying. So, he woke them up just in time for his arrest. The Jewish religious leaders stormed the garden with

a great crowd of soldiers, ready to take Jesus to stand trial and be crucified.

Jesus knew just what his mission here on earth was. Even though he told his disciples what would happen, they were surprised when Jesus was arrested, tried, and crucified. When Jesus rose from death to life, they were surprised, too. Jesus, though, was not surprised at all. You see, he came to earth to save us from our sins. Jesus knew he would take the sin of every believer on himself, that he would suffer our punishment, and that he would rise from the dead three days later. Jesus did his work on the Cross willingly, for our benefit and for his own glory.

GOD'S LEGAL DEMANDS

Paul wrote that God has forgiven the trespasses of all believers, "by canceling the record of debt that stood against us with its legal demands" (Colossians 2:14a). Our debt is a legal judgment against us, and the demands it places on us are very real. If eternal death sounds bad, that's because it is.

Have you heard John 3:16 in church? Perhaps you know it by heart. It says, "For God so loved the world, that he gave his only Son, that whoever believes in him should not perish but have eternal life." God will always be a just judge, and though people are always sinners, he loves us so much he sent his only Son to bear the legal demands of our debt.

WHO, WHAT, WHY?

VICTORY ON
THE CROSS

Once Jesus was arrested, he stood trial before the Jewish high priest, Caiaphas, and the council of elders. It seems strange that the only man who never, ever sinned would be put on trial. This trial, however, was unjust. Before the trial even began, the soldiers who arrested Jesus blindfolded him and hit him. "Prophesy!" they yelled. "Tell us who hit you!" The Bible tells us they blasphemed Jesus. To blaspheme is to act or speak against God—to slander him. It is a serious thing to mock God, and that is just what the soldiers did.

The Jewish religious leaders said, "Tell us if you are the Christ." Jesus replied that he would be seated at God's right hand. He meant he would be sitting on his throne in heaven. "Are you the Son of God—is that what you're saying?" his enemies demanded. "You say that I am," Jesus said. So, the leaders decided Jesus was guilty of blasphemy—of slandering God by saying he is God. The sad, ironic thing about this is that Jesus truly is God the Son, so the priests and scribes were actually the ones blaspheming God.

Then, the Jewish leaders brought Jesus to the governor of Judea, Pilate, to be tried for claiming to be the King of the Jews. Pilate could find nothing Jesus was guilty of, so he sent him to King Herod of Galilee. Herod dressed Jesus in the costume of a king before sending him back to Pilate, still innocent.

After more empty ceremony, Pilate sentenced Jesus to die on the Cross. A crowd of Roman soldiers harassed and mocked Jesus, taking his clothes, beating him with whips, and throwing a kingly purple robe on him. Then, they jammed a crown from sharp thorns onto his head. The soldiers spit on Jesus and hit him with a stick before forcing him to carry his own cross toward Golgotha, which means the Place of the Skull.

Jesus was so weak he could not carry his own cross, so the soldiers forced a North African man named Simon to drag it up the hill. The women who traveled with Jesus over his three years of ministry followed behind, crying. These women stayed during the Crucifixion, not wanting to leave Jesus alone in his pain.

Do you remember that 700 years earlier, Isaiah shared God's message about the Messiah's suffering in Isaiah 53:5a? He said, "But he was pierced for our transgressions; he was crushed for our iniquities." That is just what happened to Jesus. The Roman soldiers stretched his arms out on the cross and pierced his wrists with nails. Then, they arranged his feet, one over the other, and crushed his flesh as they nailed them to the cross.

The Cross changed all of history. Why? The word testament means covenant. The Old Testament—the books of the Bible from Genesis to Malachi—describes life under the Old Covenant with God. So, what's a covenant? Good question! A covenant is

an agreement, or contract, that God made with his people.

Under the Old Covenant with God, his people worshiped him at the tabernacle, and later at the temple, with yearly festivals and the sacrifice of a lot of bulls, goats, sheep, and doves. That is because God's righteous and holy nature demands that sin be paid for by the shedding of blood. Following Jesus' crucifixion and resurrection, believers live under a New Covenant with God. Jesus conquered sin and death with his once-and-for-all sacrifice for our sins. Now, we can know God and be forgiven for our sins by believing in Jesus, confessing our belief, and repenting of our sin.

So, Jesus was crucified at nine in the morning. At noon, everything went completely dark, as if the sun no longer existed. Total darkness lasted over the whole land until three in the afternoon when Jesus cried out, "My God, my God, why have you forsaken me?" This confused some of the people watching the crucifixion. "Maybe he is Elijah the prophet from long ago," they muttered. Others mocked Jesus, and one man gave Jesus a wine-soaked sponge on a stick. Then, Jesus cried out and gave up his spirit.

When Jesus' body died, the temple veil that led into the Most Holy Place ripped from the top to the bottom. That's not all. There was a mighty earthquake, so strong that rocks split right in half. That was

frightening, but it wasn't over yet. The tombs opened, and God raised many believers from the dead. They left their graves, walked into Jerusalem, and visited with many people. A soldier who was standing guard by the cross saw all of this and exclaimed, "Surely this was the Son of God!" He was right.

Now, Jesus was really and truly dead. He was buried Friday evening in the tomb of Joseph, a rich man from Arimathea. Another man named Nicodemus helped Joseph prepare Jesus' body, and the women who served Jesus followed Joseph and Nicodemus to see where Jesus was buried. On Sunday morning, these same women returned to the tomb with oil and spices to find that Jesus was really and truly raised to life.

OUR SIN NAILED TO THE CROSS

So, what does God do with that record of debt we have created through our rebellion against God? In Colossians 2:13-14, Paul says, "And you, who were dead in your trespasses and the uncircumcision of your flesh, God made alive together with him, having forgiven us all our trespasses, by canceling the record of debt that stood against us with its legal demands. This he set aside, nailing it to the cross."

That's right. When you believe in Jesus and repent of your sins, God nails the record of your debt to the Cross. Your debt to God is finished. Jesus paid for your sins, conquered sin and death, and defeated evil. Jesus is victorious over all things.

LIVING IN
GOD'S KINGDOM

Jesus told the Jewish religious leaders that he would soon be seated on his throne beside the Father. He was, of course, exactly right. After his resurrection, Jesus appeared to many witnesses—people who saw him alive and could tell others about it. He was seen alive by the Roman guards at the tomb, by the women who went to the tomb, by his disciples, and even by over five hundred believing men at one time. Then, Jesus ascended to heaven in front of his disciples.

You know that Jesus is the King of the Universe. Those of us who believe in Jesus, have confessed him with our mouths, and have turned away from our sins to follow him. If you believe in Jesus then you have been made a part of his kingdom. In fact, all believers from all nations throughout history are in the kingdom of God.

Now, until Jesus returns and institutes the new (sinless) earth, his kingdom is not yet whole. We are in a strange in-between spot. You see, believers already live in the kingdom of God as children of the King. That said, we are not yet in God's kingdom-made-whole. Instead, though Jesus is King and his people worship him, sin still remains on this earth. We do not yet see Jesus with our eyes.

On the Day of the Lord, Jesus will return to gather his people to live with him forever. As he arrives with the clouds, we will rise into the air to meet Jesus. The dead, too, will rise to life in their new forever bodies. Those of us who are still alive will be given a new forever body as well. Paul said it this way, "we shall all be changed, in a moment, in the twinkling of an eye, at the last trumpet. For the trumpet will sound, and the dead will be raised imperishable, and we shall be changed" (1 Corinthians 15:51a-52).

You remember that our sin separates us from God because he is holy and just and cannot tolerate sin. Well, when Jesus returns to make his kingdom new, clean, and whole, sin will not be a part of it. In fact, there will be an entirely new heaven and new earth where there is no pain, there are no tears, and sin is completely absent. Satan and unbelievers will be overthrown in a great judgment, and will be sent to hell, which is called a lake of fire in the Bible.

Until that day, you and I are living in God's kingdom but not his completed kingdom. God's Kingdom has not been fully made whole. So, how are we to live until Jesus returns? Once, when Jesus was telling his followers that he would suffer and be killed before rising three days later, he gave his disciples an instruction. Jesus said, "If anyone would come after me, let him deny himself and take up his cross and follow me" (Mark 8:34a).

You see, we belong to Jesus. He bought our freedom with his very own blood. When we are saved from our sins, we naturally want to glorify, which means to honor and praise Jesus in the way we love and serve both God and other people. We want to follow Jesus with our whole lives, even when it is uncomfortable.

Jesus told his disciples, "If anyone would come after me, let him deny himself and take up his cross daily and follow me" (Luke 9:23). That does not mean we will be crucified. It just means that sometimes following Jesus will involve work. Although every believer is called to make disciples and to share the good news of Jesus, we will each carry our own cross differently. When we become a part of his kingdom family, Jesus gives each believer different gifts to glorify God and to serve the other believers in God's kingdom.

Some believers will preach God's Word to his people. Other Christians will teach the Bible in writing or in Bible study. Some believers will encourage others to continue following Jesus, even when it's hard. Still other Christians are skilled at caring for people during illness, while some excel at planning and thinking ahead. Some believers find it easy to help those in need by giving money, time, or resources. There are lots of ways to serve Jesus.

Whatever it is that you are good at, you are called to glorify Jesus through your work. In Colossians 3:23-24, the apostle Paul writes, "Whatever you do, work heartily, as for the Lord and not for men, knowing that from the Lord you will receive the inheritance as

your reward. You are serving the Lord Christ." When Jesus returns, Christians will all stand before him to answer for how we have used the gifts, talents, and abilities he has given us.

Because of the Cross, believers will not have to pay for their sins, which have been forgiven. Instead, Jesus will reward those who have served him well for their faithfulness. Our good works will never save us from our sins—only Jesus could do that on the Cross. But we just may be awarded with a crown in eternity.

THE WORLD CRUCIFIED TO ME

If you have believed in Jesus, confessed your belief with your mouth, and repented of your sin, you are forgiven and saved to live eternally for Jesus. That is a wonderful gift from God that not one of us deserves. That's why Paul wrote, "But far be it from me to boast except in the cross of our Lord Jesus Christ, by which the world has been crucified to me, and I to the world" (Galatians 6:14).

It is important for us to remember that our salvation is a gift from Jesus. We are not saved because of anything good we did. Instead, we are saved because of the work Jesus did on the Cross on our behalf. When we follow Jesus, the world—all the evil things that are not of God—is crucified to us. We, in turn, are crucified to the world. We are living in the world, but we are not of the world. We are already in God's kingdom, but not quite yet living in the new earth where sin and death will be forever gone.

TIMELINE

Before 4000 BC – God creates the heavens and the earth.

Satan tempts Eve and Adam. The Fall happens and sin enters the world.

1446 BC

The Israelites celebrate the first Passover and leave captivity in Egypt. This is the early date for the Exodus.

Note: The dating for the rule of Pharaohs in Ancient Egypt varies, as calendars varied. Also, there are two widely accepted dates for the Exodus. This timeline is based on the early date. The early date of the Exodus works backward from dates in Scripture, and is supported by many conservative scholars.

c. 740-681 BC

Isaiah serves as God's prophet and writes his prophetic book, including chapter 53, a prophecy about Jesus.

c. 519 BC

King Darius the Great, the King of Persia when Ezra returned to Jerusalem, crucifies 3,000 of his political opponents in Babylon. This is the first historical reference to crucifixion.

27 BC – AD 14

Gaius Octavius is Emperor of Rome under the title Caesar Augustus.

c. 6/4 BC

Jesus is born in Bethlehem.

4 BC

King Herod dies and Judea is divided among his sons.

AD 6

The Roman Empire makes Judea a Roman province.

26

Pontius Pilate becomes the governor of Judea.

c. 27/28-29

John the Baptist ministers near the Jordan River.
- Several of the disciples, looking for the Messiah, spend time following John.
- John the Baptist baptizes Jesus.

29

John the Baptist is executed by King Herod Antipas.

c. 28-30

Jesus begins and works his public ministry, sharing the gospel, teaching disciples, and healing the sick.
- Jesus calls the Twelve Disciples to follow him.

c. 30

Jesus is crucified. He is raised from the dead and forty days later, he ascends to heaven.
- Jesus' half brother James witnesses the risen Jesus and becomes a Christian.

- Jesus sends the Holy Spirit to the believers gathered at Jerusalem and Pentecost occurs. The apostles begin to proclaim the gospel.

33/34

Jesus reveals himself to Paul on the way to Damascus and calls him to be an apostle to the nations.

36

Pilate is removed as governor due to incompetence.

37-41

Caligula is Emperor of Rome. He terrorizes Christians.

62

Paul writes Colossians while under arrest in Rome.

WORKS CONSULTED

Currid, John D. and David P. Barrett. *Crossway ESV Bible Atlas.* Crossway, 2010.

Elwell, Walter A. and Robert W. Yarbrough. "The Middle East in the Days of Jesus." *Encountering the New Testament: A Historical and Theological Survey, Fourth Edition.* Baker Academic, 2022.

Gribetz, Judah, Edward L. Greenstein, and Regina Stein. *The Timetables of Jewish History: A Chronology of the Most Important People and Events in Jewish History.* Simon & Schuster, 1993.

Grun, Bernard. *The Timetables of History, New 3rd Rev. ed.* Simon & Schuster, 1991.

Packer, J.I. *What Did the Cross Achieve?* 1974. Crossway, 2023.

Piper, John. *Fifty Reasons Why Jesus Came to Die.* Crossway, 2006.

Rhodes, Jonty. *Man of Sorrows, King of Glory: What the Humiliation and Exaltation of Jesus Mean for Us.* Crossway, 2021.

Rose Book of Bible Charts, Maps & Time Lines. Rose Publishing, 2010.

Ryle, J.C. *The Cross: Crucified with Christ, and Christ Alive in Me.* 1852. Rev. ed., Aneko Press, 2019.

Sproul, R.C. *The Truth of the Cross.* Reformation Trust Publishing, 2007.

Stott, John. *The Cross of Christ.* 1986. Centennial ed., InterVarsity Press, 2021.

The ESV Study Bible™, ESV® Bible. Crossway, 2008.

"What is the history of crucifixion?" Got Questions, https://www.gotquestions.org/crucifixion.html. Accessed April 24, 2024.

Other books in the Series

Why Did the Exodus Happen?
978-1-5271-1176-9

What was the Tabernacle?
978-1-5271-1175-2

Who was Moses?
978-1-5271-1174-5

Why Did Slavery End?
978-1-5271-1011-3

What was the Underground Railroad?
978-1-5271-1010-6

Who were the Abolitionists?
978-1-5271-1009-0

Why did the Reformation Happen?
978-1-5271-0652-9

What was the Gutenberg Bible?
978-1-5271-0651-2

Who was Martin Luther?
978-1-5271-0650-5

Who were the Disciples?
978-1-5271-1279-7

Why did the Resurrection Happen?
978-1-5271-1281-0

Who Were the Disciples?
Danika Cooley

Dive into the incredible true story of Jesus' twelve disciples – regular guys who became part of history's greatest adventure! From fishermen to tax collectors, these ordinary men were transformed into extraordinary followers who changed the world forever. With engaging black–and–white illustrations throughout, discover how Jesus' closest friends faced challenges, performed miracles, and spread the good news across the globe. Perfect for young readers who love history and adventure!

ISBN: 978-1-5271-1279-9

Why Did the Resurrection Happen?
Danika Cooley

What happened when Jesus rose from the dead that first Easter morning? This engaging book reveals how the empty tomb changed everything. Young readers will discover how over 500 people saw the risen Jesus, learn what his resurrection means for us today, and explore the amazing promise of eternal life. With vivid illustrations and clear explanations, this book brings the greatest miracle in history to life for kids ages 8–12.

ISBN: 978-1-5271-1281-0

Why Did the Reformation Happen?
Danika Cooley

The Church was following the words of men rather than the Word of God but brave men read God's Word and were saved from their sins. They fought for truth against the most powerful organizations of the time – the Church and the Crown. Danika Cooley explores how God's people changed the Church, Europe and the World. This is the story of how the Church found the gospel and the people heard about Christ.

ISBN: 978-1-5271-0652-9

Christian Focus Publications

Our mission statement
Staying Faithful

In dependence upon God we seek to impact the world through literature faithful to His infallible Word, the Bible. Our aim is to ensure that the Lord Jesus Christ is presented as the only hope to obtain forgiveness of sin, live a useful life and look forward to heaven with Him.

Our Books are published in four imprints:

CHRISTIAN FOCUS

Popular works including biographies, commentaries, basic doctrine and Christian living.

MENTOR

Books written at a level suitable for Bible College and seminary students, pastors, and other serious readers. The imprint includes commentaries, doctrinal studies, examination of current issues and church history.

CHRISTIAN HERITAGE

Books representing some of the best material from the rich heritage of the church.

CF4KIDS

Children's books for quality Bible teaching and for all age groups: Sunday school curriculum, puzzle and activity books; personal and family devotional titles, biographies and inspirational stories – because you are never too young to know Jesus!

Christian Focus Publications Ltd,
Geanies House, Fearn, Ross-shire,
IV20 1TW, Scotland, United Kingdom.
www.christianfocus.com